NORWAY
Coloring Book For Kids
With Interesting Facts

Published by Grant Publishing

Sales and Enquires: grantpublishingltd@gmail.com

FOLLOW US ON SOCIAL MEDIA

 @grantpublishingltd

GRANT
PUBLISHING

This Book Belongs To

_____

INTRODUCTION

Allow your creativity and imagination to run wild with this awesome coloring book. Bring these exciting illustrations to life while learning lots of awesome facts about Norway!

TIPS

- Don't worry if you go over the lines!
- Coloring pencils will work best, but you can also use crayons and pens to color
- Share your work with friends!
- Have fun, fun and more fun!

NORWAY
Coloring Book

CONTINENT

Norway is a country in the continent of Europe.

NAME

Norway is officially the Kingdom of Norway.

COUNTRY

Norway is made up of the mainland territory of which comprises the western and northernmost portion of the Scandinavian Peninsula and the remote Arctic island of Jan Mayen and the archipelago of Svalbard.

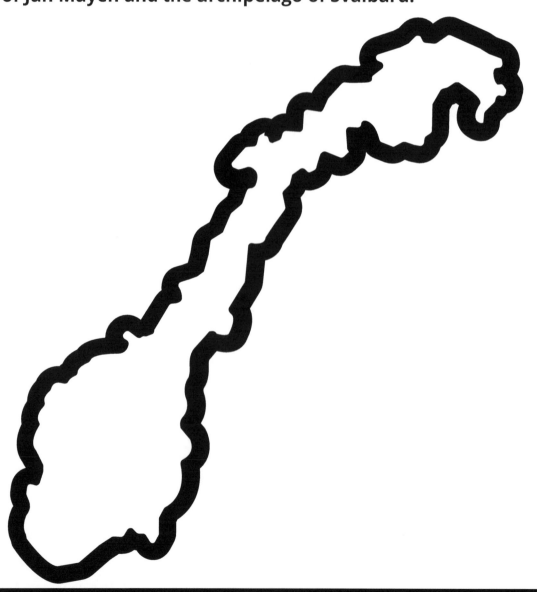

COUNTRY

Norway shares borders with Sweden, Finland, Russia, Denmark and the United Kingdom.

SIZE

Norway is 385,207 square kilometres.

CAPITAL

The capital city of Norway is Oslo.

CAPITAL

Oslo is the largest city in Norway.

CITIES

Major cities in Norway include Bergen, Trondheim, Stavanger, Tromsø and Ålesund.

POPULATION

Norway has a population of over 5 million.

POPULATION

The vast majority of the population are ethnic Norwegians.

PEOPLE

People from Norway are called Norwegian.

LANGUAGE

The official languages of Norway are Norwegian and Sámi.

LANGUAGE

Recognised languages in Norway include Kven, Romani, Scandoromani and Norwegian Sign Language.

ANTHEM

The national anthem of Norway is "Ja, vi elsker dette landet".

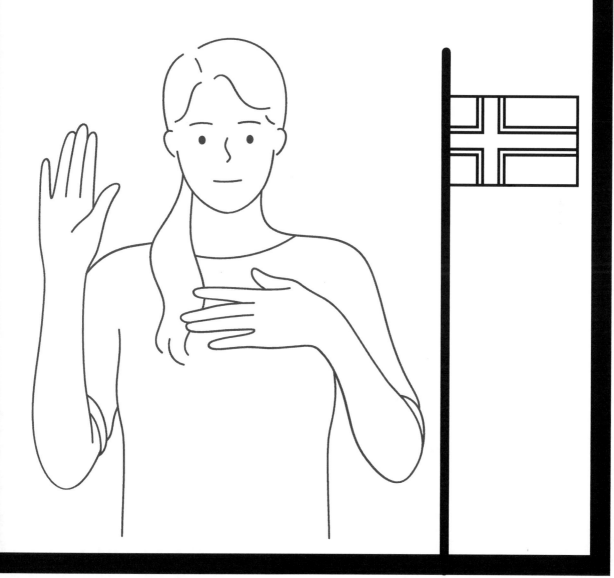

CURRENCY

The currency is the Norwegian krone.

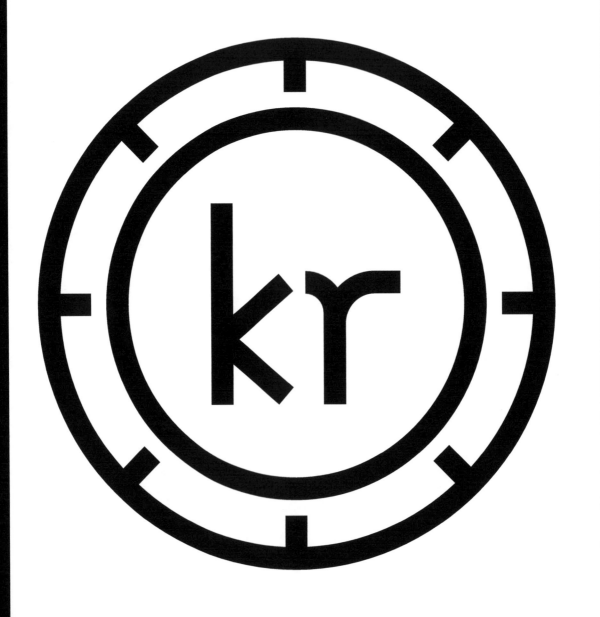

ECONOMY

Norway has the fourth-highest per-capita
income in the world on the World Bank and IMF lists.

DRIVING

In Norway, people drive on the right side of the road.

COAST

Norway has an extensive coastline, facing the North Atlantic Ocean and the Barents Sea.

RIVER

The longest river in Norway is The Glomma.

LAKES

The largest lake in Norway is Lake Mjøsa.

LAKES

Major lakes in Norway include Røssvatnet, Femunden, Randsfjorden and Tyrifjorden (Lake Tyri).

MOUNTAIN

Galdhøpiggen is the highest mountain in Norway, Scandinavia and Northern Europe.

SYMBOLS

The moose is the main national animal of Norway and the lion is Norway's national royal animal.

ANIMALS

Norway has a diverse range of wildlife which includes animals such as arctic fox, musk ox, polar bears and reindeers.

CRIME

Norway also has one of the lowest crime rates in the world.

SPORTS

Football is the most popular sport in the country.

DISHES

Fårikål is the national dish of Norway.

DISHES

Brunost, Vafler and Smalahove are popular foods in Norway.

THE END

FOLLOW US ON SOCIAL MEDIA

 @grantpublishingltd

GRANT
PUBLISHING